BIBLE STUDIES FOR LIFE
SMALL GROUPS

THRIVE

LIVING IN REAL JOY

TONY MERIDA

LifeWay Press® • Nashville, Tennessee

Thrive: Living in Real Joy
Bible Studies for Life: Small Group Member Book

© 2016 LifeWay Press®

ISBN: 9781430054948
Item: 006103914

Dewey Decimal Classification Number: 227.6
Subject Heading: JOY AND SORROW \ BIBLE. N.T. PHILIPPIANS \ CHRISTIAN LIFE

Eric Geiger
Vice President, LifeWay Resources

Gena Rogers
Sam O'Neal
Content Editors

Michael Kelley
Director, Groups Ministry

Faith Whatley
Director, Adult Ministry

Send questions/comments to: Content Editor, *Bible Studies for Life: Adults*, One LifeWay Plaza, Nashville, TN 37234-0175; or make comments on the Web at *BibleStudiesforLife.com*.

Printed in the United States of America.

For ordering or inquiries, visit *lifeway.com*; write LifeWay Small Groups; One LifeWay Plaza; Nashville, TN 37234-0152; or call toll free (800) 458-2772.

We believe that the Bible has God for its author; salvation for its end; and truth, without any mixture of error, for its matter and that all Scripture is totally true and trustworthy. To review LifeWay's doctrinal guideline, please visit *lifeway.com/doctrinalguideline*.

Bible Studies for Life: Adults often lists websites that may be helpful to our readers. Our staff verifies each site's usefulness and appropriateness prior to publication. However, website content changes quickly so we encourage you to approach all websites with caution. Make sure sites are still appropriate before sharing them with students, friends, and family.

contents

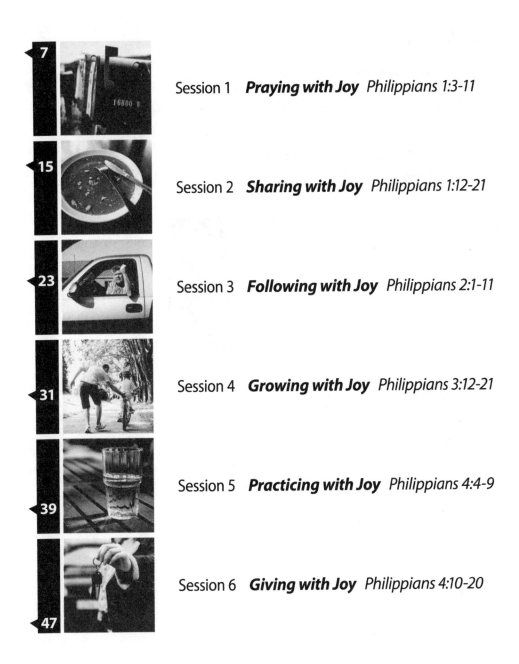

Social Media

 Connect with a community of *Bible Studies for Life* users. Post responses to questions, share teaching ideas, and link to great blog content. ***Facebook.com/BibleStudiesForLife***

 Get instant updates about new articles, giveaways, and more. **@BibleMeetsLife**

The App

Bible Studies for Life is also available as an eBook. The eBook can be opened and read with the *Bible Studies for Life App*, a free app from the iOS App Store or the Google Play Store.

Blog

At ***BibleStudiesForLife.com/blog*** you will find additional resources for your study experience, including music downloads provided by LifeWay Worship. Plus, leaders and group members alike will benefit from the blog posts written for people in every life stage—singles, parents, boomers, and senior adults—as well as media clips, connections between our study topics, current events, and much more.

Training

 For helps on how to use Bible Studies for Life, tips on how to better lead groups, or additional ideas for leading this session, visit: ***ministrygrid.com/web/biblestudiesforlife***.

ABOUT THIS STUDY

Don't just survive. Thrive!

The Book of Philippians addresses many of our deepest questions.

▶ *Where can we find full and lasting joy?* Look and listen to Paul. He radiated a contagious joy throughout his letter. Indeed, the happiest man in Rome was the apostle in prison! Paul reminds us that we don't derive ultimate joy from comfortable circumstances, but from a living, vibrant communion with Christ. Joy isn't about attaining more stuff; it's about treasuring Christ more.

▶ *Where can we find meaning and purpose in life?* Paul teaches us about a life worth living—and a death worth dying. He shows us the path to living this life by pointing us to Jesus, who provides the power and the example we need.

The Christian life isn't an easy life, but it's full. It's joyful. It's the kind of life you've always been looking for and always wanted to lead.

Of course, Jesus never promised us that life would be easy. But He did promise He would always be with us. And if He is with us, we have everything we need for joy and peace.

We can do more than just live as we follow Christ. We can thrive!

ABOUT THE AUTHOR

Tony Merida

Tony Merida is the founding pastor of Imago Dei Church in Raleigh, N.C. He also serves as Associate Professor of Preaching at Southeastern Baptist Theological Seminary in Wake Forest, North Carolina. He's the author of several books, including *Ordinary: How to Turn the World Upside Down.*

1 | PRAYING WITH JOY

When has a personal letter or note meant a lot to you?

Prayer is an opportunity to experience joy.

THE BIBLE MEETS LIFE

A few years back, Pharrell Williams launched the song "Happy" as a global sensation. But I wonder if the people singing it then have remained happy over the years. These days, perhaps many of them would prefer U2's "I Still Haven't Found What I'm Looking For."

Such people wouldn't be alone in history.

▶ King Solomon, who had an abundance of wealth and women, confessed: "Absolute futility. Everything is futile" (Eccl. 1:2).

▶ Alexander the Great is reported to have wept in his tent saying, "There are no more worlds to conquer."

▶ Tom Brady, after his third NFL championship, remarked, "There's got to be more than this."

Where can we go to find full and lasting joy?

If you're interested in finding the answer to this question, welcome to the Book of Philippians! This is a letter full of joy—interestingly, one written by a man in prison.

WHAT DOES THE BIBLE SAY?

Philippians 1:3-6

[3] I give thanks to my God for every remembrance of you, [4] always praying with joy for all of you in my every prayer, [5] because of your partnership in the gospel from the first day until now. [6] I am sure of this, that He who started a good work in you will carry it on to completion until the day of Christ Jesus.

Paul began his Letter to the Philippians—his beloved partners in the gospel—with expressions of thanksgiving, joy, and affection. Joy runs throughout Paul's letter, and the first time he used the term, he spoke of "praying with joy."

Since it's such an important concept in Philippians, let's ponder "joy" for a moment. Joy goes deeper than happiness. Our happiness is typically based on external things; it's tied to our circumstances. Joy remains with us regardless of what we have or are experiencing. We can be having a bad day, but still have joy.

We find joy in knowing Christ deeply. This may sound cheesy or elementary, but the secret to joy is in keeping our priorities arranged in this order: **J**esus, **O**thers, and **Y**ourself.

Paul exemplified a life of joy. He rejoiced in Christ despite hardship (see Rom. 5:3-5), and he lived to serve others before thinking about himself (see Phil. 2:3-4). At the core of Paul's joy was a deep love for the Savior that spilled out into love for people. Christian joy is Christ-centered and others-oriented.

Notice that we don't find Paul giving God thanks for *things*; Paul gave thanks for *people*. Paul could see evidence of God's grace in others and praised God for His work in them. In these verses, specifically, Paul was filled with joy over what God had done for the Philippians.

> *How would you describe the difference between happiness and joy?*

QUESTION #2

As part of his prayer, Paul expressed gratitude for the believers in Philippi whom he considered his partners in the gospel. This church had supported Paul and served as co-workers in the mission from the beginning of his time in Philippi. They were friends, united in Jesus and on mission together.

In verse 6, Paul gave another reason for his gratitude to God: confidence in God's nature and purposes. He was sure that God would continue—and complete—the work He had started in the Philippian believers. He based this upon his knowledge of God and his awareness of the Philippians' faith.

Don't miss the fact that God is the One who starts His work in our lives—in His grace, He initiates our salvation. But that's not the end. God always finishes what He starts in the lives of His people.

Philippians 1:7-8

7 It is right for me to think this way about all of you, because I have you in my heart, and you are all partners with me in grace, both in my imprisonment and in the defense and establishment of the gospel. 8 For God is my witness, how deeply I miss all of you with the affection of Christ Jesus.

Here we see the great emotion and warmth Paul had for the church. It's not enough to learn Paul's theology and disciplines; we also need to see how the truths he taught were evident in his life. He obviously felt and demonstrated passion in what he believed.

In verse 7, Paul said he held the Philippians in his heart. A heart-deep relationship existed between Paul and these believers (see also 2 Cor. 7:3). In Philippians 2:17, Paul said he had poured out his life for the Philippians. In this way, Paul and the Philippian believers modeled for us what it means to have Christian friendships that are centered on the gospel.

What are some obstacles that hinder us from building deeper relationships?

QUESTION #3

GIVE THANKS

Giving thanks to God is a great way to experience joy in your prayers. Use the space below to record five blessings that have brightened your life this year.

1 _____

2 _____

3 _____

4 _____

5 _____

What steps can you take to make giving thanks a more prominent part of your prayer life?

"A stranger to prayer is equally a stranger to God and to happiness."

—JOHN NEWTON

Paul said, "It is right for me to think this way about all of you." It was right because the Philippian believers were "all partners with me in grace, both in my imprisonment and in the defense and establishment of the gospel." Being a partner in grace meant more than just receiving saving grace; the Philippians also had suffered for Christ and were sharing in the struggle for making the gospel known (see 1:29-30).

Paul rejoiced because the Philippians displayed their partnership in loyalty to Paul and the mission. They not only supported Paul as he shared the gospel, but they also supported him in prayer and with financial support during his imprisonment. They didn't turn their back on Paul. They weren't ashamed of him, even though imprisonment brought great shame in that time. The Philippians' loyalty to Paul even while he was in prison made this relationship especially sweet.

As Paul pondered his relationship with the Philippians, he made a remarkable statement: "I miss all of you with the affection of Christ Jesus." He reminded them of Christ's affection for them and how God was at work in him to love them in that same way. The Greek word translated as "affection" refers to the inward parts of the body; it conveys the idea of deep compassion.

Paul was united to Christ, and because of this unity, he shared Christ's love for the church. This is a deep love that goes far beyond sentiment. It's a love we can experience, as well.

How can our group life help us build the kind of relationships Paul described in these verses?

QUESTION #4

Philippians 1:9-11

⁹ And I pray this: that your love will keep on growing in knowledge and every kind of discernment, ¹⁰ so that you can approve the things that are superior and can be pure and blameless in the day of Christ, ¹¹ filled with the fruit of righteousness that comes through Jesus Christ to the glory and praise of God.

A Christ-centered love grows in "knowledge and every kind of discernment." *Knowledge* asks the question, "What is right?" *Discernment* asks the question, "What is best?" Love leads us to live out what is both right and best. In short, a mature Christian is both biblically informed and deeply affectionate.

Why did Paul desire for the Philippians to grow in this kind of love?

▶ He desired for them to "approve the things that are superior." Paul prayed for the Philippians to choose the things that are best in this life and in their relationships. He prayed for them to have discernment in order to properly distinguish between right and wrong, between better and best, and between things that matter and things that don't.

▶ He desired for them to "be pure and blameless in the day of Christ." Jesus is coming, and we should live and pray in light of this fact.

Paul expressed this life of purity in another way: "filled with the fruit of righteousness that comes through Jesus Christ." The righteousness of God is given to the believer by faith alone (see Phil. 3:9). We are declared righteous and made acceptable to God through Christ—a righteousness that comes from outside ourselves. Just as important, out of this *position* of righteousness through Jesus, we are called to *live* righteously.

Prayer is a key element of this righteous life. Paul experienced joy as he prayed for himself and for the people he loved. May the same be true of us.

> *Why are both knowledge and discernment necessary ingredients for loving others?*

QUESTION #5

LIVE IT OUT

How will you incorporate joy into your life and prayers this week? Consider the following suggestions:

▶ **Cultivate gratefulness.** Take time each day to count your blessings. As you pray and thank God for all He's done for you, let His joy fill your heart and be seen as you serve others.

▶ **Memorize Philippians 1:6.** It's hard to be joyful when praying about a difficult matter, but Philippians 1:6 is a reminder that God is at work even when we don't yet see the result.

▶ **Partner with others.** Join with others to pray about your lives and your opportunities to serve God and others. Emphasize the importance of joy each time you pray together.

Don't buy into the lie that joy depends on your present circumstances. Paul wrote his joyful letter to the Philippians (and prayed his joyful prayers) while being persecuted in a Roman prison. Choose today to seek the unshakable joy that is only available through Christ.

My thoughts

Share with others how you will live out this study: **#BSFLthrive**

2 | SHARING WITH JOY

> *What do you like so much that it's hard to share?*

QUESTION #1

#BSFLthrive

I can share Christ with joy no matter what.

THE BIBLE MEETS LIFE

My friend Joel led a church-planting program in Kiev, Ukraine, for over ten years. He used to have a map hanging in his office that was dotted with pictures of church planters leading churches all across the former Soviet Union.

On a visit to Kiev, I showed a friend this map on Joel's wall. I pointed to Immanuel from Lithuania, a massive guy with tattoos on every finger. Immanuel once described how, while in prison, he would rip out pages of the Bible, fill the paper with marijuana, and proceed to puff away. But now, Immanuel is no longer in prison, and he no longer "smokes the Bible." Now, he preaches the Bible.

How in the world does a person go from smoking the Bible and living in opposition to the gospel to preaching the Bible and telling others about the good news of Jesus Christ? The answer is simple: Jesus changes lives. Immanuel found a far greater joy in knowing and sharing Jesus.

In the same way, Paul, once a terrorist against the church, became a joyful evangelist within the church.

WHAT DOES THE BIBLE SAY?

Philippians 1:12-14

[12] Now I want you to know, brothers, that what has happened to me has actually resulted in the advance of the gospel, [13] so that it has become known throughout the whole imperial guard, and to everyone else, that my imprisonment is in the cause of Christ. [14] Most of the brothers in the Lord have gained confidence from my imprisonment and dare even more to speak the message fearlessly.

Paul was in prison because of his ministry. But as he wrote to the Philippians, he didn't focus on his incarceration. He didn't whine about his luck. Instead, he took a divine perspective on the whole situation, reminding the church that—even while he was in prison—God's mission was being accomplished. People were being positively impacted by his imprisonment, and Christians were being emboldened.

We can learn from Paul, because this divine perspective isn't always easy to adopt. Circumstances can drain the joy right out of us. And frankly, ministry can also use up our joy. The key to maintaining joy in life and ministry is to hold onto the source of our joy. Stay focused on Jesus.

The best news for Paul was that his trials had served to advance the gospel, particularly in the political center of the world: Rome. Not only were the guards and Roman officials hearing the good news, but Paul also had been placed in the great city where his witness was impacting many others. Because he cared about the gospel more than his own comfort or his personal ambitions, he could rejoice.

Let's pray for great courage as we joyfully make the gospel known to people. If you find yourself in a great trial, you certainly should pray and seek the support of others. But also be encouraged to see hardship as an opportunity. In adversity, we get to advertise the Savior's grace. We get to testify to the gospel of Jesus!

> *When have you been encouraged by the faith and perseverance of others?*

QUESTION #2

Philippians 1:15-19

¹⁵ **To be sure, some preach Christ out of envy and strife, but others out of good will. ¹⁶ These do so out of love, knowing that I am appointed for the defense of the gospel; ¹⁷ the others proclaim Christ out of rivalry, not sincerely, seeking to cause me anxiety in my imprisonment. ¹⁸ What does it matter? Just that in every way, whether out of false motives or true, Christ is proclaimed. And in this I rejoice. Yes, and I will rejoice ¹⁹ because I know this will lead to my deliverance through your prayers and help from the Spirit of Jesus Christ.**

Paul mentioned two different motives driving two different types of evangelists:

> *What do these verses teach us about sharing Christ?*
>
> QUESTION #3

- ▶ **Envious evangelists** preached out of "strife" and "envy," driven by selfish ambition. They looked at Paul's imprisonment as an occasion to tear him down, to stir up trouble, and elevate their ministry over Paul's.

- ▶ **Empathetic evangelists** preached out of "good will," driven by love. They cared about Paul and understood he was in prison by God's sovereign will, and not as a result of Paul's disobedience or unfaithfulness.

In verse 18, we see the message mattered more to Paul than the messengers or their motives. Paul never tolerated those who preached a false gospel; in fact, he wrote his Letter to the Galatians to oppose any attempts at a false gospel. But if the true gospel was preached, then Paul could rejoice. Certainly, Paul would have preferred to have the right message for the right motives, but he placed the highest importance on the message itself.

Such a strategy still works today—proclaiming the good news to people even as we live attractive and joyful lives before them. Let's care about Jesus' glory more than our own, and let's rejoice continually until we see Him face to face.

PERSONAL ASSESSMENT: EVANGELISM

How confident do you feel in your ability to share the gospel? Use the following questions to evaluate your comfort level as a witness for Christ.

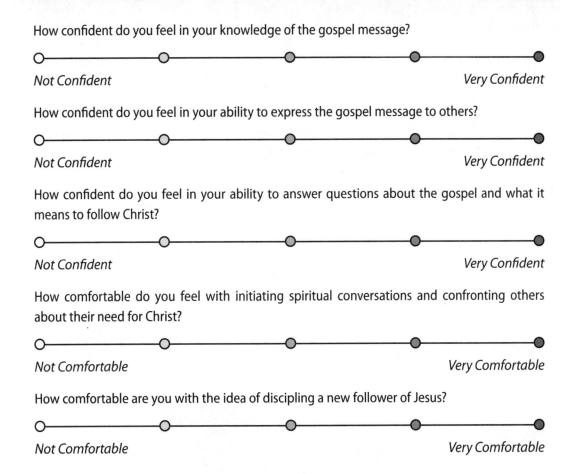

How confident do you feel in your knowledge of the gospel message?

Not Confident   *Very Confident*

How confident do you feel in your ability to express the gospel message to others?

Not Confident   *Very Confident*

How confident do you feel in your ability to answer questions about the gospel and what it means to follow Christ?

Not Confident   *Very Confident*

How comfortable do you feel with initiating spiritual conversations and confronting others about their need for Christ?

Not Comfortable   *Very Comfortable*

How comfortable are you with the idea of discipling a new follower of Jesus?

Not Comfortable   *Very Comfortable*

"It could be that one of the great hindrances to evangelism today is the poverty of our own experience."

—BILLY GRAHAM

Anyone who follows Christ should prepare for criticism. We should be ready to follow Paul's example. He didn't try to defend himself. He simply stayed focused on living his life for Christ and proclaiming the truth. He put the gospel first. You can't control what others think of you; all you can do is finish your race with faithfulness.

In verse 19, Paul revealed two things he relied on in his ministry—even while in prison. Those were the prayers of the church and the help of the Holy Spirit. May we rely on these each day!

Like Paul, we can share the gospel with joy no matter our circumstances. To do that, we need to keep it simple and focus on Jesus. We need to put the gospel first. We need to care about other people and the glory of Christ more than our own glory. And we must persist when the haters hate.

Philippians 1:20-21

20 My eager expectation and hope is that I will not be ashamed about anything, but that now as always, with all boldness, Christ will be highly honored in my body, whether by life or by death. 21 For me, living is Christ and dying is gain.

Whatever you set out to do in life, in work, or in your family, make this your plan for the future: "Christ will be highly honored in my body, whether by life or by death." Talk about a mission statement!

But Paul didn't stop there. He added in verse 21, "For me, living is Christ and dying is gain." Three things stand out about that declaration:

▶ **The public nature of the statement.** Paul was public about his ambition to live for Christ. He gladly let others see it. We show what's most important to us by how we live. Paul knew that if he continued to live, it would translate into "fruitful work" (v. 22). You can't say you're living for Christ if you're not working for Him. So if you're going to represent Him, go public!

▶ **The grace in this statement.** Paul's goal was to know Christ fully and live for Him. But as he stated in Philippians 3:12-15, he had not yet attained this goal. Paul didn't achieve perfection, but God's grace was with him. His life for Christ still resulted in "fruitful work." As with Paul, our lives flow from our union with Christ. We need His grace to represent Him. Each day, we must saturate ourselves in His grace and then resolve to live faithfully for Him before a watching world.

▶ **The steadfast attitude in this statement.** When we're living in the grace of Jesus, empowered by His Spirit, we can share Paul's unstoppable, joyful mentality. We can live courageously for Christ knowing that if we die, we will be with Him. We can't lose!

Do you see the power of this perspective? Kill me? I'll be with Christ. Let me live? I'll live for Christ. Make me suffer? I'll experience joy and get rewarded by Christ. This is the unstoppable mentality of the apostle Paul. This can be our mentality, as well, but only when we treasure Christ above all things.

How would you fill in this blank: "For to me to live is _____"? If you said "Christ," then death is gain to you. If you put money, sex, power, or anything else in the blank, then it's time to repent and make some serious changes. Nothing else satisfies, and nothing else will last.

In Christ, we can have irrepressible joy in a life worth living and courage in a death worth dying. But in Christ alone.

Why do we sometimes feel ashamed about sharing the gospel?

QUESTION #4

How can we help one another be bold in sharing the gospel?

QUESTION #5

LIVE IT OUT

We can experience great joy as we share Christ. Consider these suggestions for putting that truth into action this week:

▶ **Treasure Jesus above all.** Take a few moments to repent of desiring other things more than your Savior. Ask the Father to wean you off the pleasures of sin and this world.

▶ **Pray for people you don't ordinarily pray for.** Think about your critics, attackers, or enemies. Think about people you envy. Think about people in other churches. Pray for each of them to know Christ and to make Christ known.

▶ **Reach out to people who need the gospel.** Intentionally initiate a conversation with someone who needs Christ. Ask the Father to fill you with joy and confidence as you share the truth this week and beyond.

There are lots of people in today's world who would rather smoke the Bible than read it. That shouldn't surprise us, nor should it take away our joy. Instead, it should motivate us to get to work.

My thoughts

Share with others how you will live out this study: **#BSFLthrive**

3 | FOLLOWING WITH JOY

When have you really needed an attitude adjustment?

QUESTION #1

We can live in love and humility even as Christ did.

THE BIBLE MEETS LIFE

I went into a convenience store to grab a bottle of water. The cashier asked, "Where are you from? You don't look like you're from around here." I replied, "I live in North Carolina."

He then said, "You look like [pop icon] Pitbull. Do you know him?" I said, "Not personally, but I know who he is."

Then the pushy cashier asked, "Are you married?" I responded, "Yes, happily." To which he asked: "Why are you married? How old are you?" "I'm thirty-seven," I answered. He said: "You're too young to be married. A man needs many women."

I smiled and replied: "You need Jesus. And you need a wife."

Looking back, I wish I'd told him to read Philippians 2. In this passage, we find the right outlook on life. Specifically, life isn't about satisfying our lusts; it's about joyfully following Christ and glorifying the One who willingly gave His life for us.

WHAT DOES THE BIBLE SAY?

Philippians 2:1-2

[1] **If then there is any encouragement in Christ, if any consolation of love, if any fellowship with the Spirit, if any affection and mercy,** [2] **fulfill my joy by thinking the same way, having the same love, sharing the same feelings, focusing on one goal.**

Following Jesus isn't a solo act. We grow in Christ as we live connected to other Christ followers. In these verses, Paul gave us a four-fold motivation for unity among believers. We see these as a series of "if" statements, which we may better understand as "since" or "because" statements. The "if" in these cases refers to *certainties*, not *possibilities*.

These four motivations for Christian unity are:

▶ **The encouragement in Christ.** We have the blessing of being found in Christ and knowing Christ (see 3:9-10). In the midst of trials and suffering, we find encouragement in our relationship with Him.

▶ **The consolation of love.** Believers have experienced Christ's love, and this shared experience leads us to love each other.

▶ **The fellowship with the Spirit.** The Spirit unites us as brothers and sisters (see 1:27), partners with us in the gospel (see John 16:13-15), leads us in our service and worship (see Phil. 3:3), and helps in our weaknesses (see Rom. 8:26). Disunity threatened the Philippian congregation (see Phil. 4:2-3), so Paul reminded them of the Spirit-produced fellowship they shared.

▶ **Shared affection and mercy.** Christians share a common experience of being the objects of God's compassion. This tender care should cause us to look out for the interests of others (see Phil. 2:4).

> *Why is unity so essential in the church?*

QUESTION #2

Since the Philippian believers were motivated in these four ways, the church could carry out Paul's command to "fulfill my joy by thinking the same way, having the same love, sharing the same feelings, focusing on one goal." Paul wanted the church to be like-minded in order to complete his joy.

Paul's own well-being was tied to the unity and growth of the church, a group of people he loved so much he called them "my children" (Gal. 4:19). A parent's well-being is tied to the maturity and growth of his or her kids, and church leaders feel the same way about the church families they are called to lead.

Paul encouraged the Philippians to get their heads on straight and remember their identity and common mission as followers of Jesus Christ. His words likewise encourage us today.

We have joy as we grow together in purpose and love.

Philippians 2:3-4

³ **Do nothing out of rivalry or conceit, but in humility consider others as more important than yourselves. ⁴ Everyone should look out not only for his own interests, but also for the interests of others.**

In order for the church to experience unity, we must pursue humility. More precisely, we must pursue Christ-like humility.

The humble person will avoid "rivalry and conceit." Paul wrote earlier about the preachers who were wrongly motivated to "preach Christ out of envy and strife" or to "proclaim Christ out of rivalry" (1:15,17). Now he told the whole church it was necessary to avoid these attitudes. Every church member should be aware of the presence of rivalry and seek to put it to death immediately.

The word "conceit" is translated as "vainglory" in some Bible versions. It's an empty glory, a glory that doesn't exist. People are literally conceited over nothing! Jesus Christ demonstrates the very opposite of this. Nothing is empty about His glory. To practice humility, we must lay aside conceit and seek the glory of Jesus.

Paul told the church not just to consider their own interests, but to look out "also for the interests of others." In this age of obsessively taking and posting "selfies," a lifestyle of thinking about others seems to be rare. How can we cultivate a life of humility?

▶ **Reflect on the cross of Christ.** In Philippians 2:5-11, Paul gave us a compelling picture of ultimate humility: Jesus coming to earth as a man and willingly giving His life on the cross.

▶ **Reflect on the glory of Christ.** Verses 5-11 also point to Christ's exaltation and humanity's climactic confession and worship of Jesus. Allow Christ's all-sovereign lordship to inspire you to humbly bow and adore Him.

▶ **Reflect on God's Word.** The Bible reveals Christ. Studying the Bible can be an act of humility in itself—if you read it with an attitude that says, "I hunger for Your Word."

▶ **Look to God in prayer.** We must humble ourselves regularly before God's mighty hand and cast our cares upon Him (see 1 Pet. 5:6-7). When we pray, we humbly recognize our inability to meet our own needs.

▶ **Serve.** We grow in humility when we serve others and put the needs of others ahead of our own.

What are the consequences when people look out for their own interests in a community?

QUESTION #3

What are the benefits when people look out for one another's interests in the church?

QUESTION #4

Philippians 2:5-11

⁵ **Make your own attitude that of Christ Jesus, ⁶ who, existing in the form of God, did not consider equality with God as something to be used for His own advantage. ⁷ Instead He emptied Himself by assuming the form of a slave, taking on the likeness of men. And when He had come as a man in His external form, ⁸ He humbled Himself by becoming obedient to the point of death—even to death on a cross. ⁹ For this reason God highly exalted Him and gave Him the name that is above every name, ¹⁰ so that at the name of Jesus every knee will bow— of those who are in heaven and on earth and under the earth— ¹¹ and every tongue should confess that Jesus Christ is Lord, to the glory of God the Father.**

Want to know what humility and selflessness looks like? Beginning with verse 5, Paul pointed to Jesus as the perfect example of the mindset we need and the humility we should pursue.

Philippians 2:5-11 highlights key doctrinal truths and provides a foundation for Christian living—all within the setting of a hymn. The song draws us to both adoration and imitation. That's helpful, because the more we behold Jesus' glory and imitate His character, the more we'll be unified as a church.

This hymn not only teaches us the pattern God gave us to follow, which is Christ; it also reminds us of the power we have through the Spirit to emulate Christ. As human beings, we fail to serve God and others perfectly, but Christ died for self-absorbed, self-glorifying people like us. He rose from the dead on our behalf, and He empowers us to follow His example.

Christ's humility is stunning. As Jesus Himself said, "The Son of Man did not come to be served, but to serve, and to give His life—a ransom for many" (Mark 10:45). That's the mindset we need.

Still, don't let Jesus' humility overshadow His authority. As Paul wrote, Jesus is exalted "far above every ruler and authority, power and dominion, and every title given, not only in this age but also in the one to come" (Eph. 1:21). In other words, Jesus reigns over all—and everyone must give an account to Him.

> *How can we work together to obey Paul's command in verse 5?*

QUESTION #5

PICTURING HUMILITY

Which of the following images best illustrates your understanding of what it means to be humble. Why?

Why is humility a necessary characteristic for those who follow Christ?

"As long as you are proud you cannot know God.... As long as you are looking down you cannot see something that is above you."

—C. S. LEWIS

LIVE IT OUT

What steps can you take to reflect the humility of Jesus? Consider the following suggestions:

▶ **Ask for help.** Ask God each day to help you be more others-oriented. Pray for help to be a more joyful servant.

▶ **Memorize Philippians 2:5-11.** Paul's hymn was memorized and recited by the early Christians. We should follow their example. Write it. Meditate on it. Memorize it.

▶ **Meet a need.** Find someone in your church who needs to experience the blessing of Christian service, and humbly serve him or her this week. Remember to serve privately, and remember to choose someone who can't pay you back.

There are plenty of people in this world who will tell you how should behave. Don't listen. Instead, concentrate on developing your relationship with Christ and let Him show you the best way to live.

My thoughts

Share with others how you will live out this study: **#BSFLthrive**

> **When have you been thankful you didn't quit?**

QUESTION #1

Day by day, I can become more and more like Jesus.

THE BIBLE MEETS LIFE

Running a marathon is a grueling task in any year. But the 36,000+ runners who competed in the 2014 Boston Marathon carried something extra: the emotion of running that historic event the year after it was marred by tragedy in 2013, when two terrorists' bombs killed three people and injured 260 others.

Meb Keflezighi was one of those competitors in 2014. As he ran, he had the names of the previous year's victims written on his bib. Incredibly, Keflezighi not only finished the race—he won. In fact, he became the first American to win in 29 years. And at 38, he was the oldest person to win in over 80 years.

As he crossed the finish line, people in the crowd chanted "U.S.A." Keflezighi lifted his hands upward with joy and triumph. His hard work and endurance paid off.

In Philippians 3, Paul used the analogy of running a race to capture his passionate, all-consuming desire to pursue Christ. The apostle's desire to run hard after his Savior is a great example of how we can strive to become more and more like Jesus.

WHAT DOES THE BIBLE SAY?

Philippians 3:12-14

12 Not that I have already reached the goal or am already fully mature, but I make every effort to take hold of it because I also have been taken hold of by Christ Jesus. 13 Brothers, I do not consider myself to have taken hold of it. But one thing I do: Forgetting what is behind and reaching forward to what is ahead, 14 I pursue as my goal the prize promised by God's heavenly call in Christ Jesus.

Paul, the great apostle, knew he wasn't perfect. He had progressed in his walk with Christ, but he wasn't content to stay there. So he pressed forward, making "every effort to take hold of it" (v. 12), "reaching forward to what is ahead" (v. 13), and pursuing "as my goal the prize promised by God's heavenly call in Christ Jesus" (v. 14).

Notice Paul's use of both "forgetting" and "reaching forward." We can let go of the past when it's forgiven in Christ. Paul had persecuted Christians—some even to death (see Acts 22:4-5). But he was forgiven. He simply let go of the past, and so should we.

▶ **We should forget past failures.** It's only after we've been forgiven and sought to make wrongs right that we can forget our transgressions and run forward. Yet we must not dwell in the past. We must not let Satan accuse us when Christ has forgiven us (see Rom. 8:33-34).

▶ **Forget past achievements.** Paul occasionally recounted some of his ministry achievements (see 2 Cor. 11:22–12:4), but he didn't use past victories as an excuse to slow down in the present. In the same way, we should be grateful to God for all of His blessings and benefits, but we're not to use yesterday's struggles or victories as excuses to live complacently today.

> *What experiences or encounters have helped you grow spiritually?*
>
> QUESTION #2

> *What principles in these verses can help us pursue the goal of Christlikeness?*
>
> QUESTION #3

What about the future? How do we reach forward and pursue God's prize? Hear the simplicity of Paul's words: "one thing I do."

Paul's one thing was Jesus. He was wholly captivated by the gospel. In verse 12, he wrote, "I also have been taken hold of by Christ Jesus." In verse 14, he described "God's heavenly call in Christ Jesus," another beautiful statement about God's grace in salvation.

Paul never lost the wonder of the gospel; nor should we. All our spiritual growth comes from the outflow of our union with Christ.

Philippians 3:15-19

[15] **Therefore, all who are mature should think this way. And if you think differently about anything, God will reveal this also to you.** [16] **In any case, we should live up to whatever truth we have attained.** [17] **Join in imitating me, brothers, and observe those who live according to the example you have in us.** [18] **For I have often told you, and now say again with tears, that many live as enemies of the cross of Christ.** [19] **Their end is destruction; their god is their stomach; their glory is in their shame. They are focused on earthly things.**

Paul knew that who we choose to follow is important. He told the Corinthians to follow his example, just as he followed Jesus (see 1 Cor. 11:1). Here, he highlighted the same theme as he instructed the Philippians in how to grow up spiritually.

First, Paul encouraged Christians to adopt his outlook and values. He included himself in the phrase, "we should live up to whatever truth we have attained." Second, Paul instructed the Philippians to "observe those who live according to the example you have in us." Faithful examples included those who lived out the values Paul wrote about, such as putting the needs of others ahead of their own (see 2:3-4), not grumbling or complaining (see v. 14), and pouring out their lives for the cause of the gospel (see vv. 16-18). It's essential not only that we *hear* sound teaching, but that we also *observe* sound teaching through the lives of others.

In the same way, we should aspire to be faithful examples for others. We don't need a "position" to influence people by our example. We're already examples to our children, our neighbors, and our co-workers.

In Philippians 3:18-19, Paul offered several examples we should avoid following. He called them "enemies of the cross of Christ." Such people appear to profess some sort of Christian faith, but in reality they're pretenders, and that makes them deceivers. Enemies of the cross don't boast of what Jesus has done for them; instead, they glory in their own abilities and accomplishments. Their actions aren't consistent with their professions. And because their professions are false, Paul said, "their end is destruction."

Such pretenders are known for a particular set of values, all of which conflict with Christian holiness:

> ▶ **"Their god is their stomach."** They serve lustful appetites and seek to please self. They become a law unto themselves.

> ▶ **"Their glory is in their shame."** They show off things for which they should be ashamed.

> ▶ **"They are focused on earthly things."** They get excited about worldly things and are unable to focus on Christ, His cross, or His resurrection.

How can we intentionally position ourselves to benefit from the example of others?

QUESTION #4

Philippians 3:20-21

²⁰ **but our citizenship is in heaven, from which we also eagerly wait for a Savior, the Lord Jesus Christ. ²¹ He will transform the body of our humble condition into the likeness of His glorious body, by the power that enables Him to subject everything to Himself.**

Beginning in verse 20, Paul turned back to the mindset we should have as disciples of Christ. Specifically, we're to live in light of our true citizenship, which is in heaven.

As we grow in spiritual maturity, we realize that this world is not our home—and that we won't reach our full maturity until we reach heaven. Certain things in this life cause us to "groan within ourselves" because we aren't there yet (see Rom 8:22-23). We belong in heaven.

For this reason, our values and lives as Christ's followers should point to heaven. Through our lives here on earth, we can show others what the King is like and what His kingdom is like. Wouldn't it be great for people to observe the words and deeds of believers and say, "You aren't from around here are you?"

There's more. Believers aren't just to live out heaven's values; we also should be awaiting heaven's Lord: "We also eagerly wait for a Savior, the Lord Jesus Christ." One day, we will see Jesus face-to-face. In that moment, "He will transform the body of our humble condition into the likeness of His glorious body." Christian maturity is about growing in Christlikeness. Each day as we follow Jesus, we have the opportunity to become more and more like Him—a process that will reach its climax when Christ appears.

All this is Christ's doing. He will transform us "by the power that enables Him to subject everything to Himself." Jesus has authority over all things, including our selves. When we see Him, we won't regret pressing on to know Him more and more in this life. We won't regret living every day in view of our true citizenship.

Each day is a chance to become more like Jesus, and each is another day closer to His return. So keep going. Keep running the race until you see Him face to face.

> *What makes these verses challenging?*
> *What makes them encouraging?*

QUESTION #5

HEADING

Instead of a Driver's License, use the template below to create a "Heavenly ID." Fill in the blanks with characteristics that represent your citizenship in God's kingdom.

PHOTO

Name: _____

Date of Birth: _____

Date Born Again: _____

Spiritual Gifts: _____

_____

Mission: _____

_____

_____

"When I was a child, I spoke like a child,
I thought like a child, I reasoned like a child.
When I became a man, I put aside childish things."

—1 CORINTHIANS 13:11

LIVE IT OUT

How will you press forward to become more like Jesus in the days to come? Consider the following suggestions:

▶ **Forget what is past.** Do you have something in your past that you need to "forget" in order to run forward? Ask God to impress on you the richness of His grace and to give you strength to run today.

▶ **See others as Jesus does.** As you look at people in our culture who are not following Jesus, do you respond to them with anger? Indifference? Or, do you weep? Pray daily for God to deepen your concern for those who are enemies of the cross.

▶ **Eliminate sinful habits.** Evaluate your life for any sinful habits that restrict you from maturing spiritually. Confess the sin and be aggressive in removing this habit from your life.

You may not be able to run a marathon, let alone win one. But you can run the daily race as a disciple of Jesus. All you need to do is forget the past, focus on Christ, and keep moving forward until the day your transformation is complete.

My thoughts

Share with others how you will live out this study: **#BSFLthrive**

PRACTICING JOY

Do you typically see the glass as half-empty or half-full? Explain.

QUESTION #1

When I focus on Christ, joy and peace flood my life.

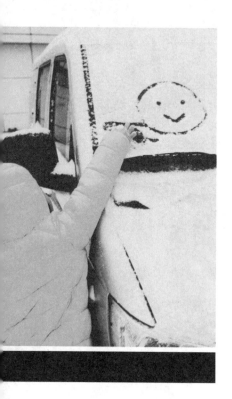

THE BIBLE MEETS LIFE

Do you have at least one problem in your life? You probably do. In fact, you may be saying, "I wish I had only one problem!"

So how do we face the multiple challenges in our lives? One approach Norman Vincent Peale popularized in the 1950s was to engage in positive thinking. Over the years, other authors and speakers have also promoted the idea Peale presented in his book, *The Power of Positive Thinking*. But is that really what we need for life?

In reality, we can't mask our problems or fix them by just "thinking happy thoughts." But we can have joy. And the presence of joy does impact how we think about and deal with life's challenges.

In this session, we'll take a peek into Paul's pastoral study—one that just happened to be in a prison cell. Bound in chains, Paul didn't engage in positive thinking; instead, he focused on Christ. In Philippians 4, Paul showed us that, when we focus on Christ, we experience joy and peace no matter what challenges we face.

WHAT DOES THE BIBLE SAY?

Philippians 4:4-5

4 **Rejoice in the Lord always. I will say it again: Rejoice!** 5 **Let your graciousness be known to everyone. The Lord is near.**

Many things can rob us of our cheer. Doubt, death, challenges at work, illness, relational difficulties, and numerous other problems can cause Christians to lose their song. But we need not lose our joy.

That's because we don't rejoice in our circumstances; we rejoice in the Lord.

As we've discussed, Paul wasn't writing this letter from a sweet beach house. He was in prison. Some of the Philippians surely remembered when, right there in their own city, Paul and Silas were beaten and imprisoned. Yet the two evangelists spent that night praying and singing hymns of praise (see Acts 16:11-25). Joy isn't about getting what you want; it's about being grateful for all you have in Christ.

Paul went on to say, "Let your graciousness be known to everyone." The word for "graciousness" carries the idea of having a gentle spirit with others. It's the opposite of being contentious and self-seeking.

Jesus displayed that spirit perfectly throughout His life and ministry (see 2 Cor. 10:1), including His attitude toward those who reviled and crushed Him (see 1 Pet. 2:23). We're called to be like Jesus, which is why Paul said in Philippians 4:5 that believers should display this gracious, gentle spirit with one another and before the watching world.

Paul then added, "The Lord is near." The apostle may have been speaking of the Lord's return, or he may have been drawing attention to the fact that God is always nearby, ready to assist us. Both are certainly true! Christ's return should cause us to want to live holy lives every day, while knowing Christ is near should encourage us to call on Him for help.

> *What's your initial reaction to Paul's commands in these verses?*
>
> QUESTION #2

Philippians 4:6-7

⁶ Don't worry about anything, but in everything, through prayer and petition with thanksgiving, let your requests be made known to God. ⁷ And the peace of God, which surpasses every thought, will guard your hearts and minds in Christ Jesus.

Paul's instructions here might catch you off guard: "Don't worry about anything." Of course, a degree of worry—more accurately defined as "concern"—is positive when it motivates us to carry out our responsibilities (see 1 Cor. 12:25; Phil. 2:20).

Negative worry is different. This kind of worry almost always deals with the future—something we don't possess. Negative anxiety can immobilize us and squeeze out our joy. Worries are like false prophets who tell us God isn't good, sovereign, or wise.

Instead of worry, we're called to pray. Paul began his Letter to the Philippians with a joy-filled prayer (see Phil. 1:3-11); now, he instructed his readers to pray in the face of anxiety.

We need to take steps to battle worry in our lives, as well:

▶ **Accept that we shouldn't have a heart filled with negative anxiety.** Paul simply said, "Don't worry about anything." Worry should no more be part of a Christian's life than gossip, envy, covetousness, or sexual sin.

▶ **Cast all of our cares upon God (see 1 Pet. 5:7).** The most basic remedy for anxiety is prayer. Paul said peace comes only through prayer. God never worries. He is in control, so we can give Him our burdens.

▶ **Pray with thanksgiving and intercession.** Paul didn't deny that we'll have hard times, but he knew we can still give thanks. We should also offer up our petitions to God when in need. We can offer our prayers and petitions confidently and "with thanksgiving," knowing God is faithful and will provide.

How does prayer help us move from worry to trust?

QUESTION #3

NEGATIVE AND POSITIVE

Use the chart below to illustrate the difference between negative worry (anxiety) and positive worry (concern). Record what each type of worry would look like in two of the following categories:

	Negative Worry	**Positive Worry**
Your finances are getting tight.	_____	_____
You had a fight with your spouse.	_____	_____
You're not satisfied in your current job.	_____	_____
One of your parents has a serious illness.	_____	_____
Your child is having trouble at school.	_____	_____

▶ **Fight anxiety by praying with faith in God's promises.** "And the peace of God, which surpasses every thought, will guard your hearts and minds in Christ Jesus." Once we pray and give our burden to God, we can be surrounded and sheltered by the peace of God.

This peace "surpasses every thought." That's one of the aspects that makes God's peace so extraordinary—you can have it when it makes no sense to have it!

And it all starts with keeping our focus on Christ Jesus.

Philippians 4:8-9

[8] **Finally brothers, whatever is true, whatever is honorable, whatever is just, whatever is pure, whatever is lovely, whatever is commendable—if there is any moral excellence and if there is any praise—dwell on these things.** [9] **Do what you have learned and received and heard and seen in me, and the God of peace will be with you.**

Finally, Paul addressed the Christian's thought life as a pathway to peace and joy. For Christians to grow in likeness to Jesus, we need a renewed mind (see Rom. 12:1-2; Eph. 4:23).

Because David knew people had to change their thinking to accomplish real change, he prayed for God to examine his thoughts: "Search me, God, and know my heart; test me and know my concerns" (Ps. 139:23).

God has blessed His church with His Word as a primary means of purifying our minds. Jesus prayed: "Sanctify them by the truth; Your word is truth" (John 17:17). We need God's Word to saturate our thoughts so that our minds may be renewed and we will be kept from grievous ways.

In Philippians 4:8-9, Paul urged the church to think on admirable things. He wanted disciples of Jesus to focus on that which is:

▶ True, not false.

▶ Honorable, not dishonorable.

▶ Just, not unfair.

▶ Pure, not obscene.

▶ Lovely, not unlovely.

▶ Commendable, not wrong.

▶ Morally excellent, not corrupt.

▶ Praiseworthy, not shameful.

Who or what comes to mind when you read the attributes in verse 8?

QUESTION #4

In addition to thinking praiseworthy thoughts, Paul also encouraged his readers to follow godly examples: "Do what you have learned and received and heard and seen in me." In other words, emulate leaders who think holy thoughts. Imitate believers who set their minds on our Creator and Redeemer. Watch them. Pay attention to their views, what they read, what they talk about, and what they value. By doing so, Paul said we will know more of God's peace.

When we focus and trust in Christ, we have peace. And when we focus and trust in Christ, we have joy. Don't miss out on either of those precious gifts.

How can we practice the things Paul taught in this passage?

QUESTION #5

LIVE IT OUT

How will you let the truths in the passage transform your life this week? Consider these suggestions:

▶ **Pray.** What are your biggest challenges right now? Make a list and pray daily about each one. As you pray, ask the Lord to grant you His peace and graciousness.

▶ **Memorize.** Memorize Philippians 4:6-7. I don't know of a better way to get a proper perspective on the challenges of life and the need to give our burdens to God than to saturate our minds with this passage.

▶ **Think.** Seek out a trusted friend who can help you be accountable with your thoughts. Specifically, what are some darker thoughts currently in your mind that need to be replaced with something more noble?

Take it from me: there's not much power in positive thinking—not the kind the world wants us to engage in, anyway. But there is power in Jesus. Just as important, we can find peace and joy when we focus our lives on Him.

My thoughts

Share with others how you will live out this study: **#BSFLthrive**

6 GIVING WITH JOY

When have you had a blast giving something away?

> *Join God in His work of giving for the benefit of others.*

THE BIBLE MEETS LIFE

Money. Most of us like to have it. Even more of us like to spend it. But we don't usually like to talk about it—especially at church.

Would it surprise you to know that most pastors don't like to talk about it either? Pastors don't want to appear greedy, nor do they want to be associated with "prosperity preachers"—those who preach that if you give more and more of your resources, God will bless you with health, wealth and prosperity.

In Philippians 4, however, we see that Paul was quite comfortable talking about money. He was comfortable living with money—and living *without* money. How could that be? Paul was content regardless of his financial situation because his contentment and ultimate joy was in Jesus Christ.

Let's move deeper into that joy as we explore some important passages from Philippians 4.

WHAT DOES THE BIBLE SAY?

Philippians 4:10-14

¹⁰ I rejoiced in the Lord greatly that once again you renewed your care for me. You were, in fact, concerned about me but lacked the opportunity to show it. ¹¹ I don't say this out of need, for I have learned to be content in whatever circumstances I am. ¹² I know both how to have a little, and I know how to have a lot. In any and all circumstances I have learned the secret of being content—whether well fed or hungry, whether in abundance or in need. ¹³ I am able to do all things through Him who strengthens me. ¹⁴ Still, you did well by sharing with me in my hardship.

Paul began this passage with an explosion of joy: "I rejoiced in the Lord greatly that once again you renewed your care for me." Paul was thrilled by the Philippians' generosity, compassion, and renewed support for him.

In verses 11-13, Paul explained Christian contentment. The Stoic philosophers of Paul's day interpreted contentment as "self-sufficiency." Paul revolutionized the idea of contentment from "self-sufficiency" to "Christ-sufficiency."

Contentment is about believing Christ is enough. Therefore:

> **Contentment doesn't depend on our circumstances.** Paul's contentment didn't increase or decrease based upon his material provision. He taught that the rare jewel of Christian contentment has nothing to do with our circumstances. It's found in Christ. We need only Him.

> **Contentment is learned.** Twice, Paul said he learned contentment. Paul knew abundance. He knew what it was like to be hosted by the wealthy Lydia in Philippi (see Acts 16:14-15). But Paul also knew hardship—extreme hardship. Lest we think he was merely blowing smoke, just read 2 Corinthians 11:24-27! Paul knew what abundance was like, but he'd also went without food and knew what it was like to sleep in the cold. He learned how to be content in both environments.

How would you describe what it means to be content?

QUESTION #2

Many athletes love to quote Philippians 4:13 for inspiration. But I can't dunk a basketball no matter how often I quote this verse! The phrase "all things" must be governed by the context—which in this case is about contentment and material possessions. "I can do all [these] things through Christ who strengthens me."

Paul was able to be content in every situation through Christ. This, then, is the secret: Christ is enough. Paul wasn't preoccupied with his situation; he was preoccupied with Jesus. When you focus on Jesus, you can be content.

> *Verse 13 is often taken out of context. How should we understand it in light of verses 10-12?*
>
> QUESTION #3

Philippians 4:15-18

15 And you Philippians know that in the early days of the gospel, when I left Macedonia, no church shared with me in the matter of giving and receiving except you alone. 16 For even in Thessalonica you sent gifts for my need several times. 17 Not that I seek the gift, but I seek the profit that is increasing to your account. 18 But I have received everything in full, and I have an abundance. I am fully supplied, having received from Epaphroditus what you provided—a fragrant offering, an acceptable sacrifice, pleasing to God.

Once we're content with our situations, we'll have freedom to give more freely. Looking at these verses, we can see three ways Paul described the Philippians' contribution to his ministry.

First, their giving represented a partnership in the gospel (see vv. 15-16). Let me state this negatively: if we aren't giving to God's kingdom, we're not partners in the gospel—we're more like consumers. Paul didn't view the Philippians as customers; he saw them as co-laborers. Most of the believers in Philippi were far from wealthy, yet they earned a reputation for giving sacrificially, generously, and cheerfully to support Paul's mission (see Acts 16–17 and 2 Cor. 8–9).

Second, Paul highlighted the spiritual and eternal fruitfulness of living a generous life: "I seek the profit that is increasing to your account." Paul wasn't joyful just because the Philippians had given him a gift. He was pleased because he knew the heavenly profit—the spiritual fruit—that would result from their actions. The apostle rejoiced to see the Philippians acting like Christians.

Paul had opened his letter by "praying with joy" because of the Philippians' consistent partnership, asking that they would be "filled with the fruit of righteousness" (1:4,11). Their generous giving was one demonstration of their partnership that would produce fruit.

Third, Paul described the Philippians' sacrifice as an act of worship. Just as the Old Testament sacrifices made a pleasing aroma that would ascend skyward, Paul described the church's sacrificial giving as "a fragrant offering" that was "pleasing to God." This was high praise, indeed. Paul identified sacrificial giving as an act of the highest possible value—an act of worshiping God.

What smells attract you? I like the aromas of a grill, a baseball field, coffee, and my bride. It may sound strange, but sacrificial obedience is a pleasing aroma to God. It brings Him pleasure.

Talk about a motivation to give! Modern Christians need to understand that we don't *have* to contribute financially to our local church or God's kingdom as a whole. We *get* to give! We have the privilege of worshiping God even as we contribute to His work of salvation and restoration in our world.

> **What are some keys to giving in a way that pleases God?**

QUESTION #4

Philippians 4:19-20

¹⁹ And my God will supply all your needs according to His riches in glory in Christ Jesus. ²⁰ Now to our God and Father be glory forever and ever. Amen.

Look at this magnificent promise: "And my God will supply all your needs according to His riches in glory in Christ Jesus." God used the Philippians to supply Paul's needs (see v. 18), and now Paul assured them that God would supply all their needs according to His infinite resources. Obviously, we shouldn't treat God as an ATM machine—something that only exists to feed our greed. But we can go to God to supply our daily needs (see Matt. 6:11).

Remember the secret to contentment? Christ is enough. Once we know that secret, we'll be able to see the connection between financial support and genuine gospel partnership. We'll understand that giving is a way we can bear fruit, store up treasures in heaven, and worship God. And we'll know that when we live in such a generous and sacrificial way, we can trust God to take care of us.

Continuing in verse 20, Paul rebounded with wholehearted praise to the Father: "Now to our God and Father be glory forever and ever. Amen." This is the appropriate response to God, who has provided for our salvation and continues to sustain us spiritually and physically.

God gave up His Son for our most desperate need. He provides for our daily needs, and He gives us joy that can't be found anywhere else in the world. Therefore, God alone gets the glory.

Paul burst into praise when thinking about the glory of the Father. I can't help but admire Paul for this. He was in prison, yet his spirit soared with a heart full of praise! We don't need bigger houses or bigger bank accounts to soar in worship. We simply need a bigger vision of God.

We will soar, too, when we ponder anew what the Almighty can do—and what He has already done! So let's join in His work by giving what we have for the benefit of others.

What sorts of needs can we expect God to supply?

QUESTION #5

ALL YOUR NEEDS

Make a list of five things you need right now. Pray about those needs each day, and then record how God meets each need whenever He does so.

Your Needs   **God's Provision**

1. _____   _____

2. _____   _____

3. _____   _____

4. _____   _____

5. _____   _____

How can you use God's provision as motivation to help meet the needs of others?

"We make a living by what we get.
We make a life by what we give."

—WINSTON CHURCHILL

LIVE IT OUT

How will you give of your resources in order to join God in His work? Consider the following suggestions:

▶ **Look for greed.** Greed isn't an easily detectable sin. Pray to God as you look through your recent bank statements. Ask: "Am I trusting in money more than Jesus? Do money and possessions bring me more joy than Jesus?"

▶ **Look for need.** What need can you meet within your local church? Look for an opportunity to bless others and be an active partner in the gospel.

▶ **Look together.** We can accomplish more for God's kingdom when we partner with others. As a group, find a way to regularly support and invest in a ministry that's changing lives and sharing the gospel in your community.

You may be uncomfortable talking about money. That's okay. But don't let your discomfort prevent you from experiencing the joy and contentment that comes with joining God in the good work of giving for the benefit of others.

My thoughts

Share with others how you will live out this study: **#BSFLthrive**

OUR NATIONAL DEBT:

1 9 2 4 3 4 3 4 2 2 2 6 7 7

YOUR Family Share 1 6 3 0 5 7

THE NATIONAL DEBT CLOCK

OUR DEBT, OUR WORSHIP

BY ERIC GEIGER

How do you respond when you discover a debt has been paid? Martyn Lloyd-Jones has been credited with wisely articulating that you do not know how to answer that question unless you know how big the debt is.

Perhaps you have enjoyed the experience of someone unexpectedly picking up the bill at a restaurant for you. Or, maybe you have gone through the drive-thru at a coffee shop and reached into your wallet to pay, only to be told by the barista, "The car in front of you has already paid for your bill." Pretty amazing experience, right?

But because the bill was relatively small, you likely did not bow down in the middle of the restaurant or chase the car down in front of you, pull the driver out of the seat, and pay him homage. You were grateful, but your response matched the size of the debt.

Of course, if someone paid the full balance of your mortgage or promised to cover your rent for life, your response would be different. The size of the debt dictates your response.

Words fail to capture the magnitude of the debt Christ paid for us. We committed holy treason against our holy God and rightly deserved the wrath of God. But Christ, in His great mercy, absorbed the wrath of God in His flesh in our place to make us right with God. He traded His righteousness for our sin and freely forgave us.

Our debt, a debt we could never pay, has been paid by the One we sinned against.

The size of our debt must dictate our response. When we fail to worship the Lord, we are failing to remember who He is and what He has done for us. When the Lord gave the command for Israel to worship Him and Him alone, He reminded them that the foundation of His command for them to worship Him was His rescue of them. God's saving mercy served as the basis for His command to worship: "I am the LORD your God, who brought you out of the land of Egypt, out of the place of slavery. Do not have other gods besides Me" (Ex. 20:2-3).

Later, when the priests in Israel failed to worship God rightly, He sent a prophet named Malachi to confront them on their lackadaisical and dispassionate worship. Three thoughts emerge from reading the confrontation in the first chapter of Malachi.

1. God will be worshiped. Because He is God, He must be worshiped. God will always be worshiped. His name will be great among the nations. "'For My name will be great among the nations, from the rising of the sun to its setting. Incense and pure offerings will be presented in My name in every place because My name will be great among the nations,' says Yahweh of Hosts" (Mal. 1:11).

Think about it. As you slept last night, another believer on the other side of the world was worshiping God. As that believer is sleeping now, you are reading and reflecting on the greatness of God. There is never a moment when He is not worshiped. Jesus said that the rocks would cry out if the people failed to praise Him. At all times, through all generations, God will be worshiped. God is in the midst of pursuing worshipers from every tribe, tongue, and nation who will worship Him. The scene in heaven has already been determined. There will be people from all nations worshiping Him through all eternity (see Rev. 5:9).

God is pursuing His own worship because there is nothing greater than God for God to pursue. There is nothing more glorious, nothing more beautiful, nothing more holy. If there were something greater than His own glory for God to pursue, then He would cease to be God. But there isn't. Jonathan Edwards wrote that God is "infinitely the greatest and best of beings. All things else, with regard to worthiness, importance, and excellence, are perfectly as nothing in comparison to Him."

2. We will worship. We don't have to be taught to worship. We are always pursuing something to love, something to honor, something to give us worth and meaning. When the Lord confronted the people in Malachi's day, He said of the sacrifices they were offering Him: "'Try offering them to your governor! Would he be pleased with you? Would he accept you?' says the Lord Almighty" (Mal 1:8, NIV).

The words could be applied, "If you offered your employer what you offered me, you would lose your job. If you offered your coach what you offered me, you would not be on the team. If you offered your spouse what you offered me, your marriage would not work." God was observing worship among His people, but it was not worship of Him.

demand us to worship Him, He would be allowing us to seek satisfaction in things that in the end will only deliver misery.

Because He has rescued us and paid our debt, He demands our worship be directed toward Him. Because He will be worshiped and you will worship, His commands for you to worship Him are good and gracious commands.

> **"Our debt, a debt we could never pay, has been paid by the One we sinned against. "**

At all times we worship. We cannot help it. Our worship is often misdirected to temporary things that cannot satisfy, to lesser things that will not quench. When we worship something else, we worship something less.

3. Thus, God's commands to worship Him are gracious invitations. The Lord confronts His people through Malachi for not worshiping and honoring Him. "'A son honors his father, and a servant his master. But if I am a father, where is My honor? And if I am a master, where is your fear of Me?'" (Mal. 1:6).

While the rebuke is strong in Malachi, it is also loving and gracious. God's command to worship is ultimately a gracious invitation. His commands to seek Him, to worship Him, and to honor Him are gracious invitations to worship the only One who can satisfy our hunger and quench our thirst. If He did not confront us in our misdirected worship of "little g" gods that fail to deliver on their promises, He would not be loving and gracious. If He did not

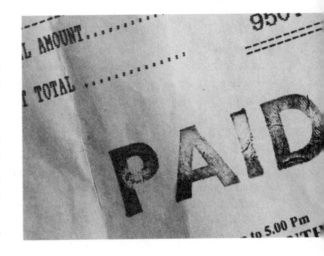

Eric Geiger serves as Vice President, LifeWay Christian Resources. Eric has authored or co-authored several books, including *Creature of the Word* and the best-selling church leadership book, *Simple Church*.

LEADER GUIDE

THRIVE

GENERAL INSTRUCTIONS

In order to make the most of this study and to ensure a richer group experience, it's recommended that all group participants read through the teaching and discussion content in full before each group meeting. As a leader, it is also a good idea for you to be familiar with this content and prepared to summarize it for your group members as you move through the material each week.

Each session of the Bible study is made up of three sections:

1. THE BIBLE MEETS LIFE.

An introduction to the theme of the session and its connection to everyday life, along with a brief overview of the primary Scripture text. This section also includes an icebreaker question or activity.

2. WHAT DOES THE BIBLE SAY?

This comprises the bulk of each session and includes the primary Scripture text along with explanations for key words and ideas within that text. This section also includes most of the content designed to produce and maintain discussion within the group.

3. LIVE IT OUT.

The final section focuses on application, using bulleted summary statements to answer the question, *So what?* As the leader, be prepared to challenge the group to apply what they learned during the discussion by transforming it into action throughout the week.

For group leaders, the *Thrive* Leader Guide contains several features and tools designed to help you lead participants through the material provided.

QUESTION 1—ICEBREAKER

These opening questions and/or activities are designed to help participants transition into the study and begin engaging the primary themes to be discussed. Be sure everyone has a chance to speak, but maintain a low-pressure environment.

DISCUSSION QUESTIONS

Each "What Does the Bible Say?" section features six questions designed to spark discussion and interaction within your group. These questions encourage critical thinking, so be sure to allow a period of silence for participants to process the question and form an answer.

The *Thrive* Leader Guide also contains follow-up questions and optional activities that may be helpful to your group, if time permits.

DVD CONTENT

Each video features Tony Merida discussing the primary themes found in the session. We recommend you show this video in one of three places: 1) At the beginning of the group time, 2) After the icebreaker, or 3) After a quick review and/or summary of "What Does the Bible Say?" A video summary is included as well. You may choose to use this summary as background preparation to help you guide the group.

The Leader Guide contains additional questions to help unpack the video and transition into the discussion. For a digital Leader Guide with commentary, see the "Leader Tools" folder on the DVD-ROM in your Leader Kit.

For helps on how to use *Bible Studies for Life,* tips on how to better lead groups, or additional ideas for leading, visit: *ministrygrid.com/web/BibleStudiesforLife.*

SESSION 1: PRAYING WITH JOY

The Point: Prayer is an opportunity to experience joy.

The Passage: Philippians 1:3-11

The Setting: The apostle Paul had established the church at Philippi on his second missionary journey (see Acts 16). It had not been one of the destinations he intended to visit, but after being prevented by God from going to some of his intended destinations, and after a pleading dream, Paul and his traveling companions arrived in the city. Then, near the end of his life and from a prison cell, Paul wrote to that church the letter we will study.

QUESTION 1: When has a personal letter or note meant a lot to you?

Remind group members that they don't have to share any details they prefer not to share when answering.

> *Optional activity:* Supplement "The Point" for this session by inviting your group to begin this study with an extended time of prayer. If your meeting space allows for it, encourage everyone to stand together in a circle. Then, ask volunteers to pray for the movement of God's Spirit in the weeks to come. Also encourage group members to lift up any requests or concerns that may be weighing them down and limiting their capacity for joy.

> **Note:** You can also lead your group in a more exuberant experience with a "concert prayer." In this method, encourage all group members to pray together at the same time, lifting up a joyful noise to God.

Video Summary: In Philippians we see that it is in Christ we find meaning, purpose, and joy for our lives. What Paul wanted more than anything was to know Christ more. He wanted to know Him in deep and profound ways. Paul lived a life of joy, but it didn't come from his circumstances. His joy came from putting Jesus first, others second, and himself last. When we life a life centered on Christ, we too will find the joy Paul talks about.

▶ WATCH THE DVD SEGMENT FOR SESSION 1. THEN USE THE FOLLOWING QUESTIONS AND DISCUSSION POINTS TO TRANSITION INTO THE STUDY.

- Where would you say you typically first look for your joy? Circumstances? Possessions? Relationships? Christ?
- Tony says, "When our hearts are happy and healthy in Christ, we minister best." In what ways have you experienced this in your own life?

WHAT DOES THE BIBLE SAY?

▶ ASK FOR A VOLUNTEER TO READ ALOUD PHILIPPIANS 1:3-11.

Response: What's your initial reaction to these verses?

- What do you like about the text?
- What questions do you have about these verses?

▶ TURN THE GROUP'S ATTENTION TO PHILIPPIANS 1:3-6.

QUESTION 2: How would you describe the difference between happiness and joy?

In order to answer this question, group members must first define happiness and joy before they move on to talk about what makes them different. If you have space in your meeting room, consider asking a volunteer to record group members' answers on a white board or large sheet of paper. Keeping a visual record is a great way to organize the group's thoughts.

> *Optional follow-up:* Where do you currently see God's "good work" in your life?

▶ MOVE TO PHILIPPIANS 1:7-8.

QUESTION 3: What are some obstacles that hinder us from building deeper relationships?

This question calls group members to examine and identify common obstacles they encounter in trying to build deep relationships with others. Through identifying these obstacles they will then be in a better position to face them when they surface again.

> *Optional follow-up:* What action steps can you take this week to remove one of those obstacles from a relationship you are trying to develop or strengthen? Be specific in your response.

QUESTION 4: How can our group life help us build the kind of relationships Paul described in these verses?

This question requires group members to identify and share specific ways their small group community can help them build meaningful relationships. It promotes accountability and reminds them of the need to act on biblical truth.

> *Optional activity:* Direct group members to complete the activity "Give Thanks" on page 11. If time permits, encourage volunteers to share what they can do to make giving thanks a more prominent part of their lives.

▶ CONTINUE WITH PHILIPPIANS 1:9-11.

QUESTION 5: Why are both knowledge and discernment necessary ingredients for loving others?

This question allows group members an opportunity to process, through the filter of the biblical text, the importance of knowledge and discernment in loving others.

> *Optional follow-up:* What steps can we take to grow in knowledge and discernment?

Note: The following question does not appear in the group member book. Use it in your group discussion as time allows.

QUESTION 6: How would you explain in your own words how joy can be found despite our circumstances, and the part prayer plays in that process?

Encourage group members to do some self-examination before they respond to this question. Then encourage them to share through the filter of their own personal experiences of finding joy in the midst of difficult times.

LIVE IT OUT

Encourage group members to consider the following suggestions of ways they can incorporate joy into their lives and prayers this week:

- **Cultivate gratefulness.** Take time each day to count your blessings. As you pray and thank God for all He's done for you, let His joy fill your heart and be seen as you serve others.

- **Memorize Philippians 1:6.** It's hard to be joyful when praying about a difficult matter, but Philippians 1:6 is a reminder that God is at work even when we don't yet see the result.

- **Partner with others.** Join with others to pray about your lives and your opportunities to serve God and others. Emphasize the importance of joy each time you pray together.

Challenge: Don't buy into the lie that joy depends on your present circumstances. Paul wrote his joyful letter to the Philippians (and prayed his joyful prayers) while being persecuted in a Roman prison. Find an opportunity this week to share with someone who is in a difficult position about a time when you were able to find joy despite hardship through your own prayers and the prayers of others.

Pray: Ask for prayer requests and ask group members to pray for the different requests as intercessors. As the leader, conclude by expressing joy at the privilege of connecting with God through prayer. Commit to taking advantage of that opportunity in the days to come.

SESSION 2: SHARING WITH JOY

The Point: I can share Christ with joy no matter what.

The Passage: Philippians 1:12-21

The Setting: This letter was written to the Christians in Philippi while Paul was a prisoner in Rome. He was under house arrest, constantly chained to a Roman guard. Although his movements were restricted, Paul considered his adversity to be a method for advancement of the gospel into unique territory. News of Paul's case before Caesar and the reasons behind it were the talk of Rome, bringing him great joy.

QUESTION 1: What do you like so much that it's hard to share?

Remind group members that their answers aren't limited to food. Other categories include technology, music, experiences, cars, and so on.

> *Optional activity:* Set the tone for this session by having a volunteer share his or her testimony of encountering Christ and experiencing salvation. Be sure to seek out the volunteer before your gathering so that he or she has time to prepare—and to make sure you don't draw a blank by asking for spontaneous volunteers.
>
> **Note:** If you aren't able to find a volunteer from your group prior to the group gathering, consider sharing your own testimony. Or, look for a volunteer outside of your regular group members.

Video Summary: "For to me to live is Christ, and to die is gain" (Philippians 1:21, ESV). This was Paul's heartbeat. Paul had joy despite hardship. Paul had joy despite conflict and criticism. Paul's heart was for Christ. One of the reasons Paul was a faithful evangelist was because he delighted in Jesus.

▶ WATCH THE DVD SEGMENT FOR SESSION 2. THEN USE THE FOLLOWING QUESTIONS AND DISCUSSION POINTS TO TRANSITION INTO THE STUDY.

- In his video message Tony asked: "What do you want? What is your greatest ambition?" How would you answer?
- Tony also said, "We talk about that which we love." What would you say your words reveal about what you love?

WHAT DOES THE BIBLE SAY?

▶ ASK FOR A VOLUNTEER TO READ ALOUD PHILIPPIANS 1:12-21.

Response: What's your initial reaction to these verses?

- What questions do you have about these verses?
- What do you hope to learn this week about sharing Christ with joy?

▶ TURN THE GROUP'S ATTENTION TO PHILIPPIANS 1:12-14.

QUESTION 2: When have you been encouraged by the faith and perseverance of others?

Inform group members that they don't have to limit their discussion to evangelism. Encourage stories of faith and perseverance from a broad range of circumstances.

Optional follow-up: When have you seen God use difficult circumstances to advance the gospel?

▶ MOVE TO PHILIPPIANS 1:15-19.

QUESTION 3: What do these verses teach us about sharing Christ?

This question requires that group members interpret the biblical text for themselves as a way to move them toward identifying what the passage says specifically about sharing Christ.

Optional follow-up: What are the basic elements of the gospel message?

▶ CONTINUE WITH PHILIPPIANS 1:20-21.

QUESTION 4: Why do we sometimes feel ashamed about sharing the gospel?

This is one of those rare moments when it may be helpful for you, as the leader, to answer the question first. If you are able to share a time when you felt ashamed or uncomfortable about sharing the gospel, you may give your fellow group members the courage they need to speak up as well.

Optional activity: Direct group members to complete the activity "Personal Assessment: Evangelism" on page 19.

QUESTION 5: How can we help one another be bold in sharing the gospel?

This question can be answered in two stages: 1) How can your group prepare or equip individuals to share the gospel? 2) How can your group work to share the gospel as a group?

Note: The following question does not appear in the group member book. Use it in your group discussion as time allows.

QUESTION 6: What emotions do you typically experience when you have the opportunity to share the gospel?

This question is designed to give group members an opportunity to share from personal experience. Don't pressure them to share if they aren't comfortable. At the same time, don't discourage them from being vulnerable if they choose to do so.

Optional follow-up: In what ways do those emotions help you share the gospel? In what ways do they hinder your efforts?

LIVE IT OUT

We can experience great joy as we share Christ. Invite group members to consider these suggestions for putting that truth into action this week:

- **Treasure Jesus above all.** Take a few moments to repent of desiring other things more than your Savior. Ask the Father to wean you off the pleasures of sin and this world.

- **Pray for people you don't ordinarily pray for.** Think about your critics, attackers, or enemies. Think about people you envy. Think about people in other churches. Pray for each of them to know Christ and to make Christ known.

- **Reach out to people who need the gospel.** Intentionally initiate a conversation with someone who needs Christ. Ask the Father to fill you with joy and confidence as you share the truth this week and beyond.

Challenge: There are lots of people in today's world who would rather smoke the Bible than read it. That shouldn't surprise us, nor should it take away our joy. Instead, it should motivate us to get to work. We know that the greatest joy anybody can experience is through a relationship with Christ. Who can *you* share that gift with this week?

Pray: Ask for prayer requests and ask group members to pray for the different requests as intercessors. As the leader, conclude by affirming your desire to share the good news of the gospel whenever opportunities arise. Ask for the Holy Spirit to guide both you and your group members in the days to come.

The Point: We can live in love and humility even as Christ did.

The Passage: Philippians 2:1-11

The Setting: Although writing from Rome while under house arrest, Paul found joy in humbly following God's plan for his life. Even while enduring confinement and uncertainty, and even while chained to a Roman guard, Paul placed the needs of the Philippians before his own. He wrote to them of the spiritual blessings we share as believers in Christ, exhorting them to turn from pleasing themselves and follow the example of Jesus in humility and obedience.

QUESTION 1: When have you really needed an attitude adjustment?

Optional activity: Ask for volunteers to role play what humility would look like in one or more of the following situations: a confrontation with a neighbor, an employee asking for a raise, or a parent correcting a rebellious teen. In each situation, assign one volunteer to play the humble person and the other to play someone angry and proud.

Note: If time permits, encourage different volunteers to play the humble person in order to reveal different ideas of what it means to express humility.

Video Summary: When we become Christians, we not only get a new Father, we get a new family. That's a wonderful privilege but it also comes with great responsibility. We are called to love and serve each other. We are called to consider others more significant than ourselves. It's not about us. It's about pointing others to Jesus. Joy comes when we turn from pleasing ourselves and turn to living humbly before God, placing the needs of others before our own. When we follow the example of Jesus in humility, we experience joy.

▶ WATCH THE DVD SEGMENT FOR SESSION 3. THEN USE THE FOLLOWING QUESTIONS AND DISCUSSION POINTS TO TRANSITION INTO THE STUDY.

- Who do you know who is an example of placing the needs of others before their own?
- How have you seen him or her live this out?

WHAT DOES THE BIBLE SAY?

▶ ASK FOR A VOLUNTEER TO READ ALOUD PHILIPPIANS 2:1-11.

Response: What's your initial reaction to these verses?

- What questions do you have about these verses?
- What new application do you hope to get from this passage?

▶ TURN THE GROUP'S ATTENTION TO PHILIPPIANS 2:1-2.

QUESTION 2: Why is unity so essential in the church?

Group members will first need to identify for themselves what unity in the church looks like. Then encourage them to articulate why that unity is so important. As time allows, you may also want to talk about what can happen when this unity isn't present, but help group members stay away from talking negatively about specific people or groups of people.

> *Optional follow-up:* What would you like to see as some common goals for your church?

▶ MOVE TO PHILIPPIANS 2:3-4.

QUESTION 3: What are the consequences when people look out for their own interests in a community?

Responses to this question can reference any community, while the discussion of Question 4 should focus specifically on the church.

> *Optional follow-up:* How would you describe the relationship between humility and unity?

QUESTION 4: What are the benefits when people look out for one another's interests in the church?

This question guides group members to focus specifically on the good that can come from unity in the church. As time permits, encourage them to share specific examples they have witnessed.

> *Optional activity:* Direct group members to complete the activity "Picturing Humility" on page 29. After volunteers share their responses, move to Philippians 2:5-11 as the ultimate picture of humility.

▶ CONTINUE WITH PHILIPPIANS 2:5-11.

QUESTION 5: How can we work together to obey Paul's command in verse 5?

This question is designed to give group members an opportunity to brainstorm specific ways they can work together to "make your own attitude that of Christ Jesus."

> *Optional follow-up:* How would you summarize the attitude of Jesus as described in this passage?

Note: The following question does not appear in the group member book. Use it in your group discussion as time allows.

QUESTION 6: How can we determine if our focus is aimed at our own significance or the significance of others?

This interpretation question will guide group members to ask themselves whether their actions line up more closely with worldly standards or God's standards.

LIVE IT OUT

What steps can you take to reflect the humility of Jesus? Encourage group members to consider the following suggestions:

- **Ask for help.** Ask God each day to help you be more others-oriented. Pray for help to be a more joyful servant.

- **Memorize Philippians 2:5-11.** Paul's hymn was memorized and recited by the early Christians. We should follow their example. Write it. Meditate on it. Memorize it.

- **Meet a need.** Find someone in your church who needs to experience the blessing of Christian service, and humbly serve him or her this week. Remember to serve privately, and remember to choose someone who can't pay you back.

Challenge: Life isn't just about us as individuals. It is about *all* of us. When we fall into selfish patterns, we don't look out for others. We can be concerned with our own interests only. Spend time with the Lord this week asking Him to help you see beyond yourself and recognize situations where you need to be others-oriented instead.

Pray: Ask for prayer requests and ask group members to pray for the different requests as intercessors. As the leader, close this time by confessing that you lack the level of humility demonstrated by Christ. Pray that God would grant each of you the courage to demonstrate strength under control as you serve His kingdom this week.

The Point: Day by day, I can become more and more like Jesus.

The Passage: Philippians 3:12-21

The Setting: Although chained to a Roman guard and awaiting trial before Caesar, Paul found joy in focusing his attention on the prize of complete spiritual maturity in Christ. He warned the Philippian believers about false teachers with worldly desires, and he exhorted them as citizens of heaven to imitate him in forgetting the past and pursuing together the goal of Christlikeness until they received the reward of glorious transformation in the presence of Christ.

QUESTION 1: When have you been thankful you didn't quit?

> *Optional activity:* Lead your group members in a brief round of light calisthenics. Ask everyone to stand up and walk in place for 30 seconds as a warm up. Then lead three or four additional exercises that are appropriate for your group members' physical condition and attire—jumping jacks, stretches, shadow boxing, lunges, jogging in place, push ups, sit ups, and so on. If you have the space, you could even allow your more competitive members to run a brief race.

> **Note:** In addition to choosing exercises that are appropriate for your group members, verbally express that any person is excused from any or all of the exercises for any reason. No one is forced to participate.

Video Summary: We can be saved in a moment, but growth in Christ is a life-long journey. Our pursuit of knowing Christ never stops. A few examples of what it looks like to pursue Christ: 1) Acknowledge that you haven't arrived. 2) Passionately pursue a greater knowledge of the Savior. 3) Never lose the wonder of the gospel. 4) Follow the right examples. 5) Live in light of your true citizenship.

▶ WATCH THE DVD SEGMENT FOR SESSION 4. THEN USE THE FOLLOWING QUESTIONS AND DISCUSSION POINTS TO TRANSITION INTO THE STUDY.

- ● What one change could you make in order to pursue the one thing that matters most?
- ● What will you do to work on making that change this week? Be specific.

WHAT DOES THE BIBLE SAY?

▶ ASK FOR A VOLUNTEER TO READ ALOUD PHILIPPIANS 3:12-21.

Response: What's your initial reaction to these verses?

- ● What do you like about the text?
- ● What new application do you hope to receive about becoming more like Jesus Christ?

▶ TURN THE GROUP'S ATTENTION TO PHILIPPIANS 3:12-14.

QUESTION 2: What experiences or encounters have helped you grow spiritually?

This question provides group members with an opportunity to share a personal story while also allowing them to identify spiritual markers from their own journey of faith.

> *Optional follow-up:* What have you always wanted to know about spiritual growth?

QUESTION 3: What principles in these verses can help us pursue the goal of Christlikeness?

Page 33 provides several possible answers to this question. Therefore, consider asking Question 3 at the beginning of your group's engagement with verses 12-14 and then lead group members through the material as a supplement to your discussion.

> *Optional follow-up:* In what ways do these verses encourage you to let go of the past and reach for what is ahead?

▶ MOVE TO PHILIPPIANS 3:15-19.

QUESTION 4: How can we intentionally position ourselves to benefit from the example of others?

This question is designed to help group members leave your session with an action plan for how they can best position themselves to learn from the example of others.

> *Optional follow-up:* What attributes should we seek out in those we allow to influence us?

▶ CONTINUE WITH PHILIPPIANS 3:20-21.

QUESTION 5: What makes these verses challenging? What makes them encouraging?

"These verses" can refer to verses 20-21, or to the entire Scripture focus for this session, which includes verses 12-21.

> *Optional activity:* Direct group members to complete the activity "Heavenly Identification" on page 37. As time allows, encourage volunteers to share their responses.

Note: The following question does not appear in the group member book. Use it in your group discussion as time allows.

QUESTION 6: We are called to follow faithful leaders. How does the impact of that truth change when you consider that someone may be following you?

This question allows group members the opportunity to consider the importance of their own actions and how they are living out their faith because others are likely watching them.

LIVE IT OUT

How will you press forward to become more like Jesus in the days to come? Invited group members to consider the following suggestions:

- **Forget what is past.** Do you have something in your past that you need to "forget" in order to run forward? Ask God to impress on you the richness of His grace and to give you strength to run today.

- **See others as Jesus does.** As you look at people in our culture who are not following Jesus, do you respond to them with anger? Indifference? Or, do you weep? Pray daily for God to deepen your concern for those who are enemies of the cross.

- **Eliminate sinful habits.** Evaluate your life for any sinful habits that restrict you from maturing spiritually. Confess the sin and be aggressive in removing this habit from your life.

Challenge: You may not be able to run a marathon, let alone win one. But you can run the daily race as a disciple of Jesus. All you need to do is forget the past, focus on Christ, and keep moving forward until the day your transformation is complete. God uses every decision, temptation, and event of our lives as opportunities to further develop His plan in and through us. In what ways can you share with others this week how and why you know this to be true?

Pray: Ask for prayer requests and ask group members to pray for the different requests as intercessors. As the leader, conclude by asking the Holy Spirit to continue your spiritual transformation. Express your desire to strain toward that goal each and every day.

SESSION 5: PRACTICING WITH JOY

The Point: When I focus on Christ, joy and peace flood my life.

The Passage: Philippians 4:4-9

The Setting: If anyone had reasons to worry, it was Paul. He was chained to a Roman guard and awaiting trial before Caesar. False teachers and opponents hounded his every step. Young churches abounded with problems. In chapter 3, he wrote of forgetting what was behind and pressing on in faith to the future. Here, he shared that focusing our lives and affections on Christ is the key to doing that with joy.

QUESTION 1: Do you typically see the glass as half-empty or half-full? Explain.

Point out the image on page 39 to help spark your group members' thoughts on this question.

> *Optional activity:* Supplement your group's discussion of Question 1 by asking those who see the glass as half-empty to stand up and walk to one side of the room and those who see the glass as half-full to walk to the other side. Once the two groups have been formed, encourage volunteers to tackle the "Explain" part of the question by elaborating on their responses.

> **Note:** If time permits, encourage volunteers to share examples of situations from their past that illustrate their tendency to see the glass as half-full or half-empty.

Video Summary: When we focus on Jesus, joy and peace flood our souls. We will have sorrow in our lives but underneath is deep, abiding joy. Anxiety and worry will weigh us down. Christians are called to center their lives in Christ, fill their minds with the things of God, and continually go to Him in prayer. The result is far different: a cause to rejoice.

▶ WATCH THE DVD SEGMENT FOR SESSION 5. THEN USE THE FOLLOWING QUESTIONS AND DISCUSSION POINTS TO TRANSITION INTO THE STUDY.

- What things cause you to be anxious?
- In his video message, Tony talks about listening "to a better sermon" when we are anxious. What "sermon" are you allowing to influence you when you start to feel anxiety? Explain.

WHAT DOES THE BIBLE SAY?

▶ ASK FOR A VOLUNTEER TO READ ALOUD PHILIPPIANS 4:4-9.

Response: What's your initial reaction to these verses?

- What questions do you have about these verses?
- What new application do you hope to get from this passage?

▶ **TURN THE GROUP'S ATTENTION TO PHILIPPIANS 4:4-5.**

QUESTION 2: What's your initial reaction to Paul's commands in these verses?

While it's usually important to give group members ample time to think through their answers to discussion questions, ask them to be more spontaneous in response to this question. You are looking for their initial thoughts after hearing these verses—their first impressions.

> **Optional activity:** Direct group members to complete the activity "Negative and Positive" from page 43. If time permits, encourage volunteers to share their responses.

▶ **MOVE TO PHILIPPIANS 4:6-7.**

QUESTION 3: How does prayer help us move from worry to trust?

This application question is intended to encourage interaction between group members and the biblical text in order to prompt discussion related to how we can move from worry to trust.

> **Optional follow-up:** When have you experienced the peace that "surpasses every thought"?

▶ **CONTINUE WITH PHILIPPIANS 4:8-9.**

QUESTION 4: Who or what comes to mind when you read the attributes in verse 8?

This question gives group members an opportunity to share with the group about someone or something that reminds them of the attributes listed in verse 8.

> **Optional follow-up:** If there is a specific person who comes to mind when you read the attributes in verse 8, in what ways has that person impacted your life?

QUESTION 5: How can we practice the things Paul taught in this passage?

Rather than offering up individual thoughts, encourage group members to work together to answer this question and to be specific in their responses.

> **Optional follow-up:** How can we help one another practice the things Paul taught in this passage?

Note: The following question does not appear in the group member book. Use it in your group discussion as time allows.

QUESTION 6: What steps can we take to rejoice even when things aren't going well?

This question requires group members to identify and share specific actions they can take to rejoice despite, and even in the midst of, difficulties.

LIVE IT OUT

How will you let the truths in the passage transform your life this week? Encourage group members to consider these suggestions:

- **Pray.** What are your biggest challenges right now? Make a list and pray daily about each one. As you pray, ask the Lord to grant you His peace and graciousness.

- **Memorize.** Memorize Philippians 4:6-7. I don't know of a better way to get a proper perspective on the challenges of life and the need to give our burdens to God than to saturate our minds with this passage.

- **Think.** Seek out a trusted friend who can help you be accountable with your thoughts. Specifically, what are some darker thoughts currently in your mind that need to be replaced with something more noble?

Challenge: There's not much power in positive thinking—not the kind the world wants us to engage in, anyway. But there is power in Jesus. Just as important, we can find peace and joy when we focus our lives on Him. Consider spending some time this week journaling. Record circumstances that seem to be robbing your peace and perspective. Then identify what you need to do to choose joy instead.

Pray: Ask for prayer requests and ask group members to pray for the different requests as intercessors. As the leader, conclude by expressing your desire to have joy and peace, even in the most difficult of circumstances. Pray that the Holy Spirit will continue transforming your heart and your mind as you serve God this week.

The Point: Join God in His work of giving for the benefit of others.

The Passage: Philippians 4:10-20

The Setting: Although Paul was under house arrest, chained to a Roman guard, and facing an uncertain future, he modeled and taught the secret of learned contentment. A tangible expression of love and support in the form of a gift from the Philippians encouraged him and provided a valuable example for us of Christ-honoring giving. Without using the phrase "thank you," Paul's words are filled with gratitude and blessing, and they culminate with praise to God.

QUESTION 1: When have you had a blast giving something away?

> *Optional activity:* Create a fun object lesson by sticking a piece of colored tape on the leg of a chair in your meeting space prior to the arrival of your group members. After discussing Question 1, announce that the person who has colored tape attached to his or her chair will receive a prize. (The prize should be something fun, like a small gift card to a coffee shop or a bag of candy.)

> **Note:** An alternate approach would be to make it so that the person with the colored tape gets to "have a blast" as the giver—he or she gets to decide who will receive the gift.

Video Summary: Within the body of Christ, believers are called to give and help others. Even as God provides for us, He calls us to be a conduit of His generosity and provision to others. We get to join God in His work by giving for the benefit of others.

▶ WATCH THE DVD SEGMENT FOR SESSION 6. THEN USE THE FOLLOWING QUESTIONS AND DISCUSSION POINTS TO TRANSITION INTO THE STUDY.

- In what ways is Jesus telling you, "Trust Me"?
- How can you share this message to help others this week?

WHAT DOES THE BIBLE SAY?

▶ ASK FOR A VOLUNTEER TO READ ALOUD PHILIPPIANS 4:10-20.

Response: What's your initial reaction to these verses?

- What questions do you have about giving for the benefit of others?
- What new application do you hope to get from this passage?

▶ TURN THE GROUP'S ATTENTION TO PHILIPPIANS 4:10-14.

QUESTION 2: How would you describe what it means to be content?

This question will give group members an opportunity to examine how their own personal definition of contentment can color the true meaning. As a follow-up to this question, consider asking group members to describe a time when they felt content.

QUESTION 3: Verse 13 is often taken out of context. How should we understand it in light of verses 10-12?

Consider using the following commentary to guide your discussion:

This secret truth was (and is) reliance on Christ through relationship with Him. Christ strengthens (the tense indicates a constant infusion of strength) the believer through relation with and complete dependence upon Him by faith. Christ is our never-ending source of power for contented living. Context is supremely important here. Power from God comes within the will of God. In the ebb and flow of life, Paul found stability in the churning waters. He depended on God's power to sustain him while in the will of God.

Optional follow-up: What are some enemies of contentment in today's culture?

▶ MOVE TO PHILIPPIANS 4:15-18.

QUESTION 4: What are some keys to giving in a way that pleases God?

Encourage group members to think practically when answering this question. What are some keys to giving as God desires in your specific community and culture?

Optional follow-up: When have you felt inspired to give above and beyond?

▶ CONTINUE WITH PHILIPPIANS 4:19-20.

QUESTION 5: What sorts of needs can we expect God to supply?

This question allows group members an opportunity to discuss, based on the biblical text, exactly what needs God has promised to supply. Encourage them to move beyond the obvious response of "all" and be specific with their answers.

Optional activity: Encourage group members to use the activity "All Your Needs" on page 53 as a journal over the coming weeks. Encourage them to keep the group informed as God meets their needs.

Note: The following question does not appear in the group member book. Use it in your group discussion as time allows.

QUESTION 6: When has God met your needs in a surprising way?

This question provides group members with an opportunity to share a personal story which also encourages the building of biblical community within the group.

Optional follow-up: Why was it surprising to you?

LIVE IT OUT

How will you give of your resources in order to join God in His work? Invite group members to consider the following suggestions:

- **Look for greed.** Greed isn't an easily detectable sin. Pray to God as you look through your recent bank statements. Ask: "Am I trusting in money more than Jesus? Do money and possessions bring me more joy than Jesus?"

- **Look for need.** What need can you meet within your local church? Look for an opportunity to bless others and be an active partner in the gospel.

- **Look together.** We can accomplish more for God's kingdom when we partner with others. As a group, find a way to regularly support and invest in a ministry that's changing lives and sharing the gospel in your community.

Challenge: You may be uncomfortable talking about money. That's okay. But don't let your discomfort prevent you from experiencing the joy and contentment that comes with joining God in the good work of giving for the benefit of others. Spend time this week asking God for eyes to see opportunities to share the resources He has blessed you with.

Pray: As the leader, close this final session of *Thrive* in prayer. Thank God for the privilege of studying His Word throughout this resource. Conclude the study by praising God once again for the opportunity to experience the kind of joy that only comes from serving Him.

Note: If you haven't discussed it yet, decide as a group whether or not you plan to continue to meet together and, if so, what Bible study options you would like to pursue. Visit *LifeWay.com/smallgroups* for help, or if you would like more studies like this one, visit *biblestudiesforlife.com/smallgroups.*

Join the conversation

Bible Studies for Life is online!
There are lots of ways to interact with people around the world
who are going through the same Bible study as your group.

facebook.com/biblestudiesforlife

Interact with other group leaders and members. Ask questions.
Share stories. Get helpful links to additional resources.

@biblemeetslife

Follow us to stay up to date with our latest blog articles and other
Bible Studies for Life news. You can also respond to discussion
questions by using hashtags that go along with each session, such
as #BSFLpeace, or creating hashtags just for your group.

My group's prayer requests